Top Ten (10) Science & Technology Trends: Beyond 2022

OWOEYE OLUWATOBI (TOBI) M.

HANDSONLABS SOFTWARE ACADEMY

Top Ten (10) Science & Technology Trends: Beyond 2022

Notice of Liability

The information in this book is on an "As Is" basis, without warranty. Neither the author nor Handsonlabs Software Academy/TOBIMICHIGAN.com shall have any liability to any person or entity with respect to any loss or damage caused or alleged to be caused directly or indirectly by the instructions contained in this book or by the computer software and hardware products described in it;

Trademarks

Handsonlabs Software Academy and Tobimichigan are trademarks or registered trademarks Incorporated in the Nigeria/United States and/or other countries. Product names, Organizations and services identified throughout this book indicates an editorial fashion only and for the benefit of such companies, organizations with no intention of infringement of the trademark. No such use, or the use of any trade name, conveys endorsement or other affiliation with this book.

ISBN: 13: 9798416825003
ISBN –10:   798-41-682-50-03

About this publication

Certain developing science and technological trends have been evolving in in recent times and their use and awareness is changing fast. Hence, the need for some professions. Among these and of the many, are **Top Ten (10) Science & Technology Trends: Beyond 2022.**

Specific Audience

This publication will be useful for undergraduates, graduates, postgraduates, and research students who want to stay updated about these trends and are willing to tailor themselves towards an ever-changing futuristic labor market.

Requisites

It is recommended that the reader be open minded and pick keynotes that can be further expounded into their area of interest or expertise so much as to be better prepared for these *inevitable* industrial changes and revolutions. Page 53 to 80 are free spaces to jot down your notes from reading this book.

Copyright & Disclaimer

DEDICATION

…To the Kingdom of Heaven and Salvation of Mankind, the reason why the Son of Man came to seek and save the Lost

TABLE OF CONTENTS

List of Figures

ACKNOWLEDGEMENTS

Firstly, I acknowledge God the Father, Son and the Holy Spirit this triune Holy entities that quietly runs the affairs of not just the entire Universe, beyond the knowledge of man, but stay atop of the very issues that has evaded the intelligence of man and its kind on earth.

Everlasting Glory, honor, and praise be to one the LAMB of God that sits upon the throne, the great I AM. To HIM BE BLESSING, GLORY HONOR AND PRAISE.

Besides, I thank Lagos State University Staff and Students that I have interacted with over the past decade. Truth said, working here in this citadel of higher learning has taught me many things.

I also thank my immediate and extended Family members who have supported me through the thick and thin periods in life.

PREFACE

Science in an extensive experience existed earlier than the current technology and in lots of notable human development. Modern technology is wonderful in its technique and a success in its results, so it now defines what technology is within the strictest experience of the term. Science in its authentic experience turned into a phrase for a form of understanding, in place of a specialized phrase for the pursuit of such understanding.

 In particular, it turned into the form of understanding that humans can speak to every different and share points. For instance, understanding approximately the operating of regular herbs turned into accumulated lengthy earlier than recorded chronicles and brought about the improvement of complicated summary concept. This proves that with the aid of using the development of complicated calendars, strategies for making toxic flora edible, and public works at a countrywide scale, together with the ones, which harnessed the floodplain of the Yangtse with reservoirs, dams, and dikes, and homes together with the Pyramids. However, no steady consciousness difference turned into made among understanding of such matters, which can be proper in each community, and different styles of communal understanding, together with mythologies and prison systems. Metallurgy turned into acknowledged in prehistory, and the Vinča way of life turned into the earliest acknowledged manufacturer of bronze-like alloys. It is concept that early experimentation with heating and combining of materials over the years advanced into alchemy.

The most primitive roots of technology links to Ancient Egypt and Mesopotamia in round 3000 to 1200 BCE, though Biblical records of the Jewish book, "Tora", as well as *recent* archaeological findings indicate much earlier times. Even though the phrases and ideas of "technology" and "nature" had been now no longer a part of the abstract view on the time, the significant Egyptians and Mesopotamians made contributions that might later locate an area in Greek and medieval technology: Mathematics, Astronomy, and Medicine. Starting in round 3000 BCE, the historic Egyptians created cutting-edge a numbering device that became decimal in individual and had oriented their information of geometry to fixing sensible issues, which include the ones of surveyors and builders. They even advanced a reliable calendar that contained 12 months, 30 days each, and 5 days on the give up of the year. Based at the scientific papyri written during the 2500-1200 BCE, the historic Egyptians believed that ailment became particularly due to the invasion of our bodies through evil forces or spirits. Thus, further to painkiller treatments, rescue treatment options might contain prayer, incantation, and ritual respectively.

Additionally, the Human Genome Project comes about in 2003, figuring out the series of nucleotide base pairs constituting human DNA, revealing and plotting all the genes of the mortal genome. Induced pluripotent stem cells advances have been on the rise since 2006, a generation permitting grownup cells to transform into stem cells able to giving upward thrust to any lining kind observed in the physical body, probably of big significance to the sector of regenerative health remedy.

While acting experiments to check hypotheses, scientists can also additionally have a desire for one results over another, and so its miles essential to make sure that technology as an entire can remove this bias. This comes with the aid of using cautious experimental design, transparency, and an intensive peer overview manner of the experimental consequences in addition to any conclusions. After the consequences, testing begins or published its miles regular exercise for impartial researchers to double-test how the studies changed into applications, succinct observation with the aid of using comparable experiments to decide how reliable the consequences would possibly be. Taken in its entirety, the clinical technique lets in for fantastically innovative trouble fixing whilst minimizing any consequences of subjective bias at the part of its users (particularly the affirmation bias).

Meanwhile, Technology involves the totality of any tactics, capacities, systems, and lines used within the industrial of products or offerings or within the accomplishment of objectives, consisting of clinical investigation. Technology may be the information of strategies, approaches, and the like, or it placed in in machines to permit for operation without targeted information in their workings. Systems (e.g. machines) making use of generation with the aid of using taking an input, converting it in keeping with the system`s use, after which generating final results are called cohort structures or technological structures. The only shape of generation is the improvement and use of fundamental gear. The prehistoric invention of fashioned stone gear observed with the aid of using the invention of the way to manipulate hearth place expanded reasserts of food. Developments in earliest times, such as the printing press, the telephone, and the Internet, have lessened bodily boundaries to communique and allowed people to engage freely on an international scale. Technology has numerous paraphernalia. It has helped broaden extra superior economies (such as today`s international economy) and has allowed the upward push of a amusement class. Many technological approaches produce undesirable with the aid of using-merchandise referred to as pollutants and use up herbal sources to the detriment of Earth's surroundings. Novelties have continually enthused the standards of a civilization and elevated new queries within the morals of generation. Instances consist of the upward push of the insight of performance in phrases of human efficiency, and the challenging situations of bioethics.

Several texts and students have provided many descriptions. A certain diction provides a differentiation of the time: by referring to technology application in relevant industry made with the aid of using generation. "The Practice, the manner we do matters round here", Ursula Franklin, (1989). The time refers to mean a particular area of generation, or to consult excessive generation or simply patron electronics, in place of generation as a whole. One writer (Bernard Stiegler), describes in this manner: as the hunt of being with the backing of using procedure aside from actuality, and as "*organized inorganic matter.*"

The difference between scientific expertise and Technological engineering era is not constantly clear. Science appears to be methodical proficiency of the bodily or cloth global won thru critical thinking and research. Technologies are not generally solely merchandise of technological proficiency, due to the fact they must fulfill necessities together with utility, usability, and safety. Engineering is the goal-orientated manner of designing and making gear and structures to make the most herbal phenomena for sensible human means, regularly (however now no longer constantly) the usage of outcomes and strategies from technological knowledge. The improvement of Technology can also additionally draw upon many fields of expertise, along with clinical, engineering, mathematical, linguistic, and historic expertise, to acquire a few sensible result. Technology is typically a consequence of industrial expertise and engineering, even though latter as human development precedes the two fields. For example, technological expertise may look at the movement of electrons in electric conductors through the usage of already-present gear and expertise. This new-discovered expertise can also additionally then serve engineers to create new gear and machines together with semiconductors, computers, and different sorts of superior era. In this sense, scientists and engineers share a common ground.

OWOEYE, Oluwatobi (Tobi) M.
https://ng.linkedin.com › oluwatobi-tobi-owoeye-15a6181b
For: Handsonlabs Software Academy
February 2022.

Chapter 1.
Next-gen Computing

The abundance of Internet of things (IoT) and 5G advancements will prod financial action and contribute $1.2-2 to worldwide Gross domestic product by 2030. The accessibility and network will drive changes across enterprises like digitalized producing, circulated energy delivery, and remote patient monitoring.

Fig. 1.1. 5G Network

<u>Image Credits: pexels.com</u>

Imagine a world in which vehicle issues are a reference to the past; to the extent that health conditions like diabetes are controlled round the clock without glucose fluctuations.

We are at the precipice of entering headway that changes the real condition of our overall population. 5G and IoT advances are spanning beyond the current Wi-Fi dispensation. This tends to a basic shift within side the mobile computing environment and could initialize billions of extra relationship over the coming 5 years

According to the GSMA, 5G network communication forecasts to make from 10 million on the in 2019 to 1.eight billion through 2025, and we are at this point at a remarkable point of achieving this feat!

Furthermore, 5G is anticipated to give speedier, extra dependable and more secure internet exchanges that power the all out from self-supporting motors to sharp frameworks for economic power and PC based insight engaged robots in assembling plants. This tremendously improves IoT climate creating an opportunity where Firms and organizations can serve billions of related contraptions with the proper trade off among speed, lethargy and cost.

Fig. 1.2. Interconnectivity of 5G Network

Image Credits: pexels.com

However, 2G came around with voice and data; 3G become generally voice, data, and information; 4G become the aggregate in 3G at any rate speedier; and 5G can be extensively faster; it will likely be provide a full-period HD film with better resolutions with time. Additionally, it is quicker in downloads; with high-pace accessibility, extraordinarily low inaction or downtimes, and widespread security will coordinate insightful vehicles and transportation foundation far reaching of related vehicles, trucks, and transports.

Besides, 5G will break the frontiers in health delivery, as well as science and engineering endeavor ushering in new possibilities.

CHAPTER 2

Distributed Infrastructure

This involves of the underlining virtual structural framework built on physical computational systems distributed in various geographic regions of the world, which can be serve in the extreme remote places in the world.

Fig. 2.1. The concept of A Distributed Architecture

Image Credits: Pexels.com

These contributions clear up varieties among stage conditions.

For instance, on the Open Systems Interconnection Model, there are transport interfaces including transport layer freedom (TLI), which permits a replacement of a few socket level-informing contributions under utility programming.

Fig. 2.2. Intelligent Network Switches, RJ45 Cables form the backbone of Distributed Systems

Image Source: Pexels.com

As everything about innovation enhances its ancestors, additional applications, modified into utility programming, encapsulated within the fundamental foundation becomes the saddled norm of advancement.

Fig. 2.3. Interoperability comes on Distributed computing with disparate Operating systems, which produces high performance computing

Image Credits: Pexels.com

One impact of this developing level of sophistication is the absence of control of the fundamental local area data in qualities of contributions that have been much uncovered on the more noteworthy crude levels.

Hadoop is a typical instance of a distributed framework created by the Apache Foundation, which permits clients to foster circulated programs without first understanding the fundamental intricacies.

Fig. 2.4. Mobile & Desktop computing needs also benefits from Distributed Computing Infrastructure

Image Credits: Pexels.com

Clients can actively exploit rapid growing entries or groups of inbound/outbound data capacities. Hadoop executes a disseminated document framework called the Hadoop Appropriated Record Framework (HDFS) intended for organization *with* minimal expense.

Chapter 3.

Automation Processing and Advancing Virtualization Technology

Distributed computing design is a way for IT Firms to guarantee that their applications constantly placed on the engineering principles that gives the best exhibition. Without a doubt, current framework apparatuses, for example, compartments and APIs have opened up numerous new engineering prospects.

Fig. 3.1. A robotic Arm with trained model intelligence that picks objects accurately

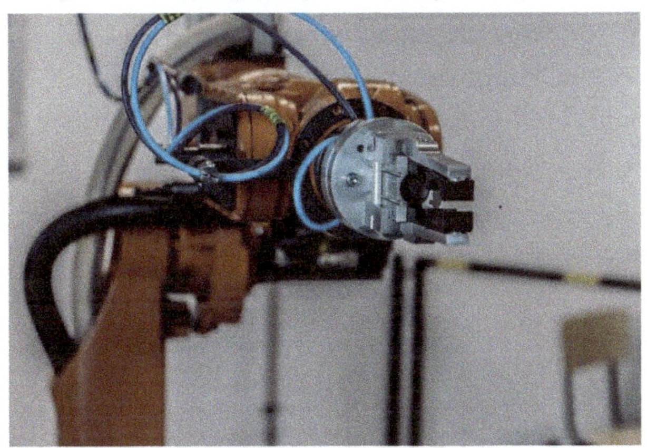

Image Credits: Pexels.com

This reminds one of facilitating applications for on-premises server farms, public mists, and edge areas. Nonetheless, this degree of foundation adaptability presents new IT the new set of technical hitches.

Fig. 3.2. Artificial Intelligence will take the chunk out of most human based tasks in the future

Image Source: Pexels.com

The current industrial revolution built on Artificial intelligence will break the frontiers of organizational needs beyond just mere local area network. This will ultimately place the administration of conveyed framework with high level of precision of common tasks.

Fig. 3.3. Intelligent Machines such as these are becoming ubiquitous in handling complex task

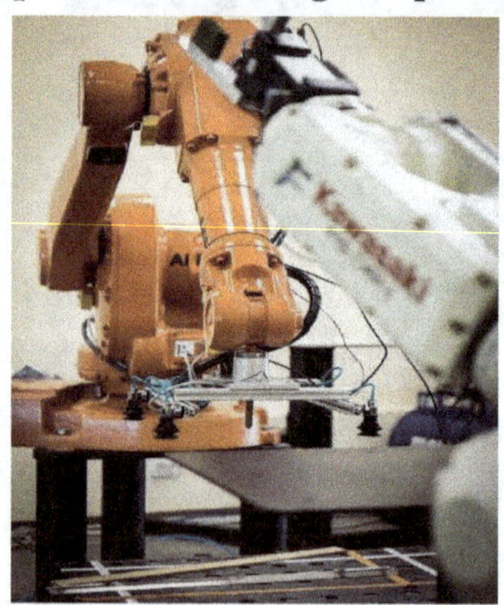

Image Source: Pexels.com

Sadly, numerous advances in administration stages actually treat the site as a divided store. Cloud reception will proceed at an amazing speed, with 70% of efforts completely relocating to the cloud or half-breed cloud beyond 2022.

CHAPTER 4

Applied AI

Applied Artificial Intelligence insight is the piece of *synthetic mental ability* that salvages it from the lab and into this current reality, engaging laptops and PC controlled robots to execute veritable computations.

Fig. 4.1. Autonomous (Driverless) Vehicles is already being tested in Arizona (USA), Shanghai (China) as well as parts of Europe like Germany

Image Credits: Pexels.com

Applied Artificial Intelligence based knowledge redesigns programming applications and puts advanced real time machine learning to use, giving obvious levels of precision and variety after some time. Applied AI is contextualizing strategies and industry processes, similarly as additional fostering the way where we interact with everything around us.

Fig. 4.2. Artificial model of Human brain Genome currently by Deep (Reinforcement) Learning built by accurate models is paving pathway for software self-orientation, intelligent assembly and self-awareness of machines.

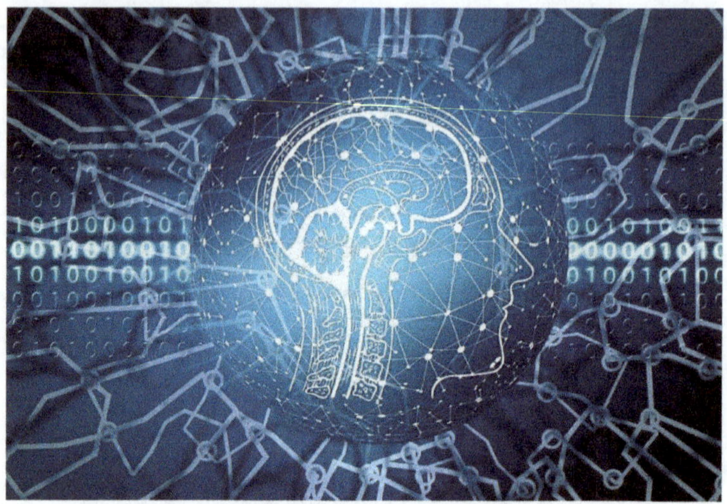

Image Source: Pexels.com

Benefits of applied artificial intelligence to daily devices include but not limited to based insight business benefits: Fast route: based on real time analytics and insight engages "human-like" judgment to decrease errors and predict high accuracy results, achieving beginning to end process automation and further developing canny contraption conditions.

CHAPTER 5
Future of Software Programming

Computer software developers are people who shape up system engineering hard/software processes. They make essentially all that we use in *say, a* virtual world. They form code, make applications and automate most of the tedious underlying that might a much longer period. It is now certain that real machines in this manner will be accept a crucial part in human activity in our future.

Fig. 5.1. Showing an excerpt of WordPress codex built on the popular PHP Web scripting Language

Image Credits: Pexels.com

It is imperative to state here that there is not point of advancing technology without syntactic codes to run and manage it, computationally. The possible advances of PC programming looks solid, yet the destiny of language machine based intelligence innovation will jump into what has to come.

Fig. 5.2. Screenshot of JavaScript, CSS Algorithm in action

Image Credits: Pexels.com

By 2024, Language machine based intelligence software algorithm processes will add to half of all human-PC collaborations. As they become more modern, they will perceive designs in our lives and expect our necessities even before we "feel" them.

Software Engineering Forecast: It is not an understatement that some software programming tasks people do now might become obsolete soon.

Fig. 5.3. Cascading Style sheets (below) now undergoing automations by several software package frameworks

Image Credits: Pexels.com

The first thing that comes to mind in Web programming is WordPress, WIX in addition, other ready to use frameworks for web development are already taking over Web programming. This is just the tip of an iceberg. Regardless of the way that we are not at that stage the current second, it is normal sense to fathom that Firms are looking for something like this. Accepting you examine history, whenever there was a prerequisite for something, this becomes apparent.

Fig. 5.4. Several Software Programming Languages face some Level of extinction in the nearest future.

Image Credits: Pexels.com

Again, it is essentially normal sense to say that the inevitable destiny of PC programming could be dreadful for programmers who are not really gifted. However, I can say that some parts of these frameworks also have spaces that skilled software engineers might be needed in the future to fix.

Possible relevant Computer Science Languages to watch out for beyond 2022

Python: Python is a versatile programming language that licenses you to make anything from application to destinations. Presumably, the greatest benefit of python is the expansive assist you with getting from the neighborhood. You can use libraries like Django and Cup to help you in your web headway needs. On a comparable hand, you can in like manner use relative libraries like Tensorflow, keras and scipy to help you in projects associated with data science.

On top of this, the ease and adaptability of python make it quite possibly the most awe-inspiring programming vernacular to learn. It is a remarkable spot to start upskilling yourself as a programmer.

R: R is to some degree more confounding than your typical programming language. As a matter of first importance, it is a bunch based multi-perspective programming language. The strong aspect of R is that it similarly fills in as an environment for plans. Comparative as python, R similarly goes with many libraries to help your knowledge. Libraries like ggplot, tidyr help you make solid applications with a negligible part of the time spent. Coming up next are three helpful characteristics of R as a programming language.

Java: Java has been the fundamental programming language for making everything from net applications, synthetic machine based intelligence novelty will move into what has to come. By 2024, manufactured machine based intelligence created discourse will add to half of all human-PC collaborations. As they become more modern, they will perceive designs in our lives and expect our necessities even before we "feel" them. Estimations, games and application side servers. It is comparative as the unheard top of all programming lingos. Yet again, the obliging neighborhood java simplifies it to encourage complex applications quickly. Various programmers use libraries like Jsat, JAVA ML, Weka and Adams to design applications for simulated intelligence.

SCALA: Scale is a superb programming language that unites the brilliance of Thing arranged programming and helpful programing into one language. Scala is a JVM language that helps programmers with making significantly versatile structures that perform incredibly complex endeavors without any problem. Firms like LinkedIn and AT&T use scale to make everything from complex artificial intelligence estimations to web applications.

C#: C# is an open source, object arranged programming language that unexpected spikes popular for the .NET construction. Designers to make colossal heaps of web applications and games used this gadget. C# was extensively used to make web and workspace applications for phones that used a Windows working framework.

Kotlin: Kotlin is a software programming language whose mechanisms operates on the Java Virtual Machine. This syntax-based language is wonderfully notable among android developers taking note of its interoperability limits between java; which makes it very easy to grasp and apply into android development tasks. It's usually advisable to go to where your capacities will pay off. Software Engineers are creative with the spur of the moment skill in critically applying computational solutions to existing problems. This is why computer science and software engineering careers will still hold huge relevance for decades to come. . Some of the useful jobs that can be done with skills in programming include but not limited to: Engineer Publicizing, Bargains engineer, Future Jobs for Software Engineering skills will include: Quality affirmation engineer, Test engineer, Business Agent, Scrum Master, Devops Developer, Data analyst, Cyber Security Inspector.

Despite the fact that some areas of software programming will not be relevant in the near future, there remains a great deal of prospective areas to explore and to be creative with in a productive manner. Motorization, artificial intelligence and computerized reasoning will plan for one more kind of programming environment later on. This inevitably will prepare for less programmable needs in a picture-perfect environment.

It is not compulsory that we as a whole can become designers; rather it is just needful to be forward thinking and use this possible forecast to grasp possibility of future trends. As previously stated, software programmers are the people who shape up the future. Since software engineers bring to life mind-concept ideas to the real world applications used day-to-day, it would be beneficial that relevance in a full Artificial Intelligence compliant environment where their usefulness might be less needful with relevant mitigations.

However, most technology innovations always require some level of algorithms to administer it. Despite the fact that the future for software engineers has good prospects, present advances made to machine learning processes such as deep learning, computer vision and other Artificial Intelligence steps clearly show that their need for tasks will drastically reduce.

Researchers decipher information investigation showed on a computerized projection.

As per the U.S. Agency of Work Measurements (BLS), programming engineers have a solid work viewpoint. The work development rate for the calling will rise up to 24% - multiple times as rapid as the usual for all professions - somewhere in the range of 2016 and 2026. Just about 302,500 positions that are open to programming engineers in the US.

Patterns in the Fate of Programming: To assist you with acquiring a superior comprehension of where IT-and PC related positions are going, a few patterns in the fate of writing computer programs insight in the accompanying areas, alongside the abilities that product improvement experts need to adjust and remain on the front line of their fields.

Software Programming of Things to come: Programming designers and other PC related experts should know about the current top programming dialects. Writing computer programs runs society's machines as a whole; everything from cell phones to traffic signals to heart screens modified with coding. Learning and utilizing programming dialects is a fundamental piece of a product engineer's work.

As previously stated, some of the software engineering Languages that might be relevant in the future are Go, Kotlin, Python, TypeScript, R, Scala, Quick, Rust, Ruby, and Haskell, as announced by TechRepublic. Capability or progressed abilities in these programming dialects would lift an expert's specialized capacities beand possibly open up more open doors when searching for job prospects.

Cross-Stage Improvement: As per TechBeacon.com, software engineers need to turn out to be knowledgeable in cross-advancement applications: Adobe, Xamarin, Appcelerator, iFactr, Kony, SAP, Alpha, 5app, FeedHenry, and Sencha, Synthetic machine based intelligence (artificial intelligence).

The eventual fate of programming additionally incorporates synthetic machine based intelligence (synthetic intelligence). Venture Technique Gathering (ESG) research uncovers that 12% of organizations use artificial intelligence based security investigation broadly while 27% use simulated intelligence put together security Synthetic machine based intelligence innovation will jump into what's to come. By 2024, synthetic machine based intelligence created discourse will add to half of all human-PC collaborations. As they become more modern, they will perceive designs in our lives and expect our necessities even before we "feel" them. With respect to a restricted premise. Simulated intelligence joining is ready to totally change the IT and PC businesses, as synthetic intelligence turns out to be progressively equipped for managing episode location, prioritizations, re-mediations, programming weaknesses, danger insight, and hazard evaluation.

Software engineers can utilize synthetic intelligence strategies, for example, AI and profound learning, to foster programming for network security. Over the long haul and innovation develops to such a postgraduate education, computer based intelligence might be the main reasonable method for managing the resulting network safety dangers. These worries are the reason the tech business is employing experts with innovative computer based intelligence innovation information to secure its organization resources.

Machine based intelligence innovation will jump into what has to come. By 2024, synthetic machine based intelligence created discourse will add to half of all human-PC collaborations. As they become more modern, they will perceive designs in our lives and expect our necessities even before we "feel" them. As per an ESG article, AI advances can be overall "applied to existing security protections as assistant applications" or "work on an independent premise combined with other security and examination advances." To remain in front of the large changes simulated intelligence will bring, software engineers and designers need to guarantee that they have what it takes fundamental for progress, for example, information on computer-based intelligence, AI, and network safety investigation.

Plan for a Vocation in the Eventual fate of Programming: Innovation's quick movement demonstrates how significant it is for experts in the IT and PC businesses to continually refresh their coding, improvement, and plan innovation abilities. More deeply study the programming dialects of things to come, cross-stage advancement, and simulated intelligence applications investigated

McKinsey sees an upheaval in programming and calls it Software 2.0. AI (ML) and computerized reasoning instruments will become brilliant enough to compose code and make new programming, and these advances will make waves in the IT business.

CHAPTER 6
Trust Architecture (Cybersecurity)

If you have not bought my book on "Internet Fraud Advisory" Fig. 6.1., I think you need just to make sure you do to have a good digest of Cyber Security Essentials.

More recently, *Zero Trust* has become one of online insurance's most used popular vocalizations. It is fundamental to get what Zero Trust is, similarly, as what Zero Trust is not.

Fig. 6.1. Internet Fraud Advisory: A Handbook on Cyber Security Essentials

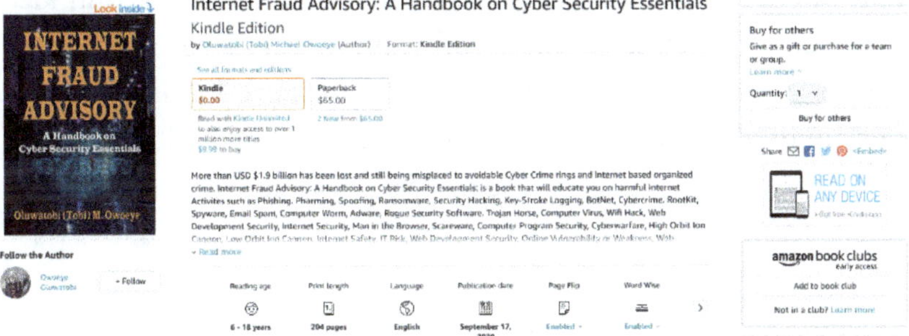

Image Source: Amazon.com

Additionally, Zero Trust is a fundamental method for managing network assurance that gets a relationship by discarding inferred trust and diligently supporting each period of a high-level joint effort. Set up in the standard of "never trust, reliably affirm," *Zero Trust*" is planned to guarantee present day conditions and enable electronic change by using strong affirmation strategies, using network division, thwarting equal turn of events, giving Layer 7 peril balance, and enhancing granular, "least access" approaches.

Zero Trust made taking into account the affirmation that standard security models work on the old assumption that everything inside an affiliation's association should be trusted. This inferred trust suggests that once on the association, customers - including risk performers and malevolent insiders - move at the edge and access or exfiltrate sensitive data because of a shortfall of granular security controls.

Fig. 6.2. Cybersecurity an essential part of Web applications

Image Credits: Pexels.com

With innovative change accelerating as a growing workforce, continued with migration to the cloud, and the difference in wellbeing assignments, embracing a Zero Trust system has never been more fundamental. At whatever point done precisely, a Zero Trust configuration achieves higher as a rule levels of wellbeing, yet also in reduced security complexity and practical vertical.

In Zero Trust, one of the underlying advances is the unmistakable evidence of an organization's largely essential and huge data, assets, applications and organizations. This spotlights on where to start and engages the creation of Zero Trust security game plans. By recognizing the most fundamental assets, affiliations can focus in tries on zeroing in on and guaranteeing those assets as a component of their Zero Trust adventure.

Zero Trust Design: Zero Trust has become one of network safety's most utilized trendy expressions. It is basic to get what Zero Trust is, just as what Zero Trust is not. It is an essential way to deal with online protection that gets an association by wiping out understood trust and consistently approving each phase of an advanced cooperation.

Established in the guideline of "never trust, consistently confirm," Zero Trust is intended to secure present day conditions and empower advanced change by utilizing solid verification techniques, utilizing network division, forestalling sidelong development, giving Layer 7 danger avoidance, and improving on granular, "least access" strategies.

With computerized change speeding up as a developing half breed labor force, proceeded with movement to the cloud, and the change of safety activities, adopting a Zero Trust strategy has never been more basic. Whenever done accurately, a Zero Trust engineering brings about higher by and large degrees of safety, yet additionally in diminished security intricacy and functional upward.

Perceivability and Basic Resource ID: In Zero Trust, one of the initial steps is the ID of the organization's generally basic and significant information, resources, applications and administrations. This focuses on where to begin and furthermore empowers the production of Zero Trust security Internet Infrastructure. By distinguishing the most basic resources, Firms can zero in endeavors on focusing on and ensuring those resources as a component of their Zero Trust venture.

The subsequent stage understands who the clients are, which applications they are utilizing and the way that they are associating with decide and uphold strategy that guarantees secure admittance to your basic resources.

Building The Zero Trust Undertaking: Albeit Zero Trust is normally connected with getting clients or use cases like Zero Trust Organization Access (ZTNA), an exhaustive zero trust approach includes Clients, Applications and Framework. Clients - stage one of any Zero Trust exertion requires solid validation of client character, use of "least access" Internet Infrastructure, and check of client gadget honesty. Applications - applying No Trust to applications eliminates verifiable trust with different parts of utilizations when they converse with one another. An essential idea of Zero Trust is that applications can't be relied upon and nonstop checking at runtime is important to approve their conduct.

Nevertheless, it is important to know that 2021 was one of the most awful years for network safety. However, later on, Firms and states will depend on inventive innovations like block-chain to foster more grounded network safety designs. What is a Zero Trust Architecture: Zero Trust has become one of cybersecurity's most used buzzwords. It is imperative to understand what Zero Trust is, as well as what Zero Trust is not.

Zero Trust is a strategic approach to cybersecurity that secures an organization by eliminating implicit trust and continuously validating every stage of a digital interaction.

Moreover, it is also based on the realization that traditional security models operate on the out-of-date postulation that everything inside an organization's network should be covertly trusted. This understood trust indicates that once on the network, users – together with threat actors and malicious insiders – are free to move laterally, access or tap on sensitive data due to lack of granular safety controls.

The growth of digital applications and devices has introduced new challenges that require system wide restrictions in order to stop the exponential threat of cybersecurity, and the transformation of security operations, taking a Zero Trust approach has never been more critical. If done correctly, a Zero Trust architecture results in higher overall levels of security, but also in reduced security complexity and operational overhead.

Visibility and Critical Asset Identification: In Zero Trust, one of the first steps is the identification of the network's most critical and valuable data, assets, applications and services. This helps prioritize where to start and enables the creation of Zero Trust security policies. By identifying the most critical assets, organizations can focus efforts on prioritizing and protecting those assets as part of their Zero Trust journey.

33

CHAPTER 7

Bio Revolution

The convergence of related fields of biology will usher in a new era of biological revolution with forward-looking promises such as gene therapy, hyper-personalized drugs, and more. Naturally, they will pose an ethical dilemma and government intervention for subsequent standardization of life science research.

Fig. 7.1. Genetically modified plants

Image Source: pexels.com

Food, energy and attire materials for an enormous scope for the better produced with Biotechnology, for the fact that it holds incredible potential past the making of antibodies, and applied needed by human body as a formidable defense system.

<u>Fig. 7.2. 3D Microscope: sample inundated with bright evenly Powerful light sources, such as lasers, are seeing greater pinpoint details</u>

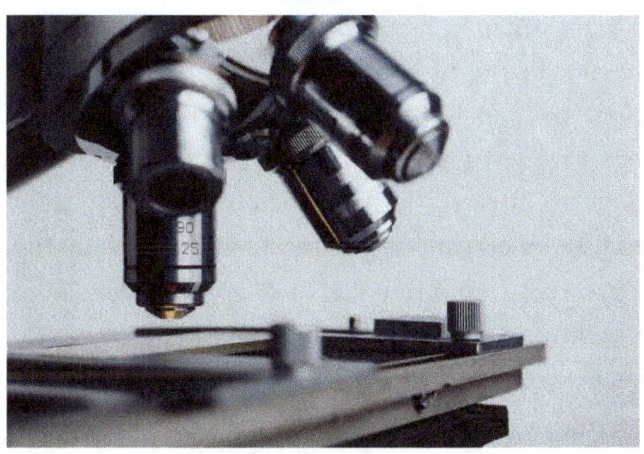

<u>Image Source: pexels.com</u>

Its true capacity is impossible without worldwide coordinated effort, including at a political level. It is imperative to consider and accelerate logical advancement around here. Ten Nobel has appreciated efforts in natural chemistry Prizes in Science towards the investigation of synthetic cycles inside and connecting with living creatures.

<u>Fig. 7.3. 3D DNA research and discovery has successfully linked human ancestry as far back as thousands of years</u>

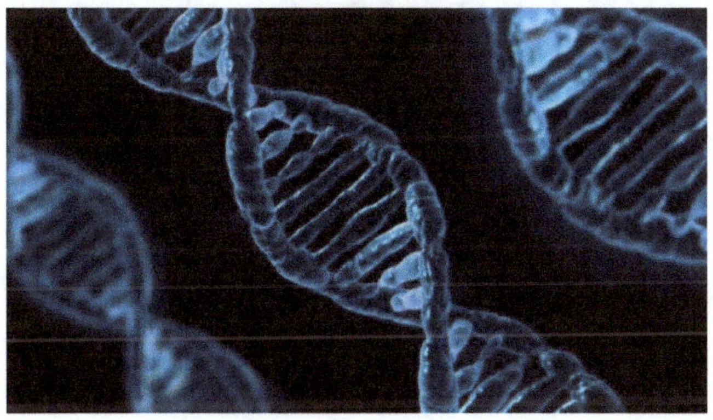

<u>Image Source: pexels.com</u>

How we might interpret genomics, sub-atomic engines and the altering of qualities, along with progresses in nanotechnology and simulated intelligence are at an unequaled high. Add to this the quickly falling expenses of a similar innovation and you have a powerful mix.

This blend is going to be both groundbreaking and exceptionally problematic across many pieces of our lives. Very much like the climb of natural science at the turn of the nineteenth century, our expanded zeroed in on proteins is presently making the bio-unrest. The intermingling of related areas of science will introduce another period of natural upset with forward-looking guarantees like quality treatment, hyper personalized medications, and that's just the beginning. Normally, they will represent a moral issue and government intercession for ensuing normalization of life science research.

The intermingling of related areas of science will introduce another period of natural upset with forward-looking guarantees like quality treatment, hyper personalized medications, and that is just the beginning. Normally, they will represent a moral issue and government intercession for ensuing normalization of life science research.

Fig. 7.4. Synthetic heart or artificial heart

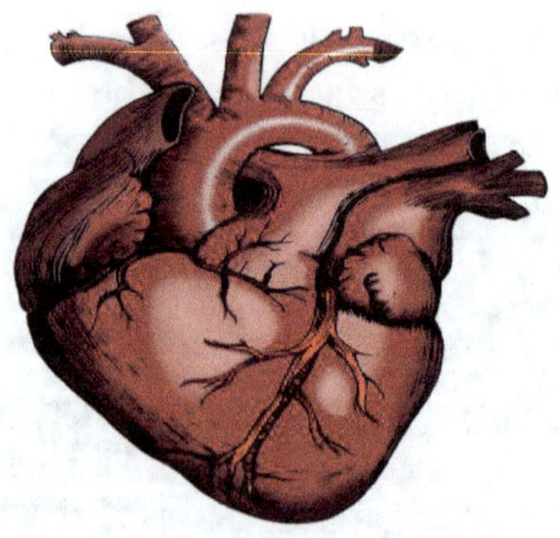

Image Source: pexels.com

As related fields in biological science converge, they will usher in a new era of bio-revolution, with futuristic promises like gene-therapies, hyper-personalized medicines, and more. Naturally, they will also raise ethical dilemmas and subsequent government-intervened standardization of research in biosciences.

Top Ten (10) Science & Technology Trends: Beyond 2022

dilemmas and subsequent government-intervened standardization of research in biosciences.

CHAPTER 8
Next-gen Materials

Inventive materials with expanded usefulness can further develop the energy efficiency of U.S. industries. Materials with novel properties will empower energy reserve funds in energy-serious cycles and applications and will make another plan space for sustainable power age.

Fig. 8.1. Touch screens are forms of Bio-Inspired Devices

<u>**Image Credits: iStock Photos**</u>

Cheaper Materials for Energy Frameworks: The turn of events and assembling of materials that proposition worked on practical properties for minimal price can reduce the expense of completed items considerably. Models incorporate cheaper photovoltaic materials and wind framework parts, electrochemical and flimsy film materials, refractories and protection materials, and materials for heat exchangers or other materials. Nanotechnologies And Materials include but are not limited to: Quantum Hydrogen on Graphene.

Superomniphobic materials: Built on water messes with that float on fluid surfaces, these materials repulse both sleek and watery liquids.

Auxetic materials: When extended, auxetic materials become thicker opposite to the applied power. This happens because of their pivot like designs, which flex when extended. Auxetics might be helpful in applications, for example, body protection, pressing material, knee and elbow cushions, strong shock retaining material, and wipe mops.

Biomaterials: Either got from nature or incorporated in the research facility, biomaterials utilized to upgrade or supplant normal capacities in the body. Currently used to a little degree, future biomaterials have the capability of further developing medication conveyance (by allowing expanded medication discharge) or to further develop uniting in transfers.

Meta-materials: Materials with an exact shape, calculation and game plan which can influence light and sound in unpredictable habits. Potential applications are assorted, including far off aviation applications, foundation observing, savvy sunlight based power the board, public wellbeing, working on ultrasonic sensors, and in any event, safeguarding structures from tremors.

<u>**Fig. 8.2. Bio-inspired super liquid repellency**</u>

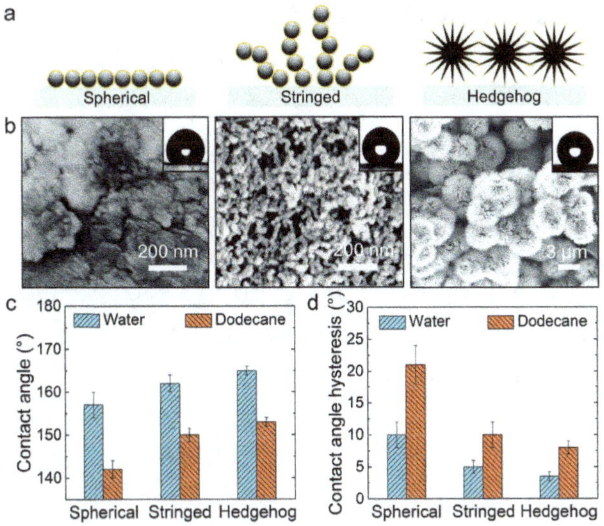

<u>**Image Credits: 1. Sarma et al (2021)**</u>

Nanoelectromechanical frameworks (NEMS): This has gone through conceptual framework in 2016, accepted in 2016 and commercially viable in 2025. Electronic materials coordinating electrical and mechanical usefulness on the nanoscale. NEMS regularly incorporate semiconductor like nanoelectronics with mechanical actuators, siphons, or engines, and may accordingly shape physical, natural, and compound sensors.

Self-recuperating concrete: Self-configuration materials is still being conceptualized up to 2023, testing has been slated in 2025 and commercially viable in 2027: These are a class of savvy materials that have the basically fused capacity to fix harm brought about by mechanical utilization over the long haul. The motivation comes from natural frameworks, which can recuperate subsequent to being injured. A material (polymers, ceramics, and so on) that can naturally address harm brought about by typical utilization could bring down creation expenses of various different modern cycles through longer part lifetime, decrease of shortcoming after some time brought about by debasement, just as forestall costs caused by material disappointment.

Machines that control individual particles with living **resembling self-recreating capacities** has been verified for use as at 2016, rolled out for use in 2018, and monetarily commercial able as at 2019.

These base up, molecularly exact 3D printers would have the option to make Internet Infrastructure of DNA, RNA or protein.

Nanofactories: A proposed framework in which *nanomachines* would join responsive particles through *mechanosynthesis* to fabricate bigger, molecularly exact parts has been project for 2023, 2024, and commercially availed in 2025. The situating instruments will collect data of expanding size to fabricate plainly visible (human-scale) items that remain molecularly exact. Disclosures in materials science, for example, nanotechnology, will assist with making new materials with extraordinary properties, from strength, weight, adaptability, and conductivity to warm assimilation.

CHAPTER 9

Clean Energy Tech

Clean energy and energy efficiency priorities will dominate all industries and drive the development of green transport, energy efficient buildings and sustainable technologies. The cost of clean energy technologies will decrease, making them available to more and more people. Extensive reception of environmentally friendly power innovations will assist the worldwide local area with controlling environmental change speed increase. RTI Global is at the front line of sustainable power execution and electric area research both locally and universally.

Fig. 9.1 shows a solar panel street light

Image Credits: https://pexels.com

Illustrations of clean energy novelty: Clean energy progressions are maintainable, less naturally intrusive approaches to driving the environment. Probably the most widely recognized instances of clean energy sources incorporate sun oriented, wind, water, geothermal, bioenergy, petroleum gas, and atomic power.

<u>Fig. 9.2 [A] Solar powered parking lot could be cost-effective</u>

<u>Image Credits: https://pexels.com</u>

Clean energy is a basic part to practical advancement all through the world. Clean energy innovation not just works on our personal satisfaction by lessening air and water contamination; it additionally mitigates energy reliance by making sustainable assets in nearby networks. It is imperative to state here that clean energy innovations are recyclable, eco-friendly and introduces pathways of mitigating the impact of global warming events. Solar, wind, water geothermal bio-infused energy sources, natural gas and nuclear energy sources are some major examples.

The significance of hygienic energy technology in sustainable development increases daily as it produces efficient, environmentally spotless energy, which is a critical component to sustainable development throughout the world. Clean energy technology not only progresses our quality of life by plummeting air and water pollution, it also alleviates energy want by creating renewable resources in local societies. Overreliance on single fuels add to energy insecurity and enormous climate change consequences.

Fig. 9.2 [B] Solar powered parking lot could be cost-effective

Image Credits: https://pexels.com

Scaling Renewable Energy Technology and Electricity Grid Integration: Fostering an Enabling Environment for Renewable Energy in the future comes with the aid of wind and sunlight based are fueling a spotless energy revolutions. This is what you want to know about renewables and how you can assist with having an effect at home. The fact is that Sustainable power is lasting, as development cuts down expenses and begins to follow through on the guarantee of a spotless energy future. American sunlight based and wind age are breaking records and integrated into the public power framework without compromising unwavering quality.

This infers that renewables are progressively removing "filthy" non-renewable energy sources in the power area, offering the benefit of lower outflows of carbon and different sorts of contamination. Biomass and huge hydroelectric dams make troublesome tradeoffs while considering the effect on natural life, environmental change, and different issues. This is what you should be familiar with the various kinds of environmentally friendly power sources-and how you can utilize these arising innovations at your own home.

Environmentally friendly power, regularly talked about to as perfect energy, comes from normal sources or cycles that are continually renewed. Daylight or wind are energy sources that useful into energy saving trails.

<u>Fig. 9.2 [C] Solar powered parking lot could be cost-effective</u>

<u>Image Credits: https://pexels.com</u>

Solar Power is environmentally friendly power and is a revered innovation, bridling nature's power utilized for warming, transportation, lighting, and other relevant applications. Wind has controlled boats to cruise the oceans and windmills to crush grain. The sun has given warmth during the day and fueled flames to endure the night.

Since we have progressively imaginative and more affordable ways of catching and hold wind and sunlight based energy, renewables are turning into a more significant power source, representing more than one-eighth of U.S. age. The extension in renewables is additionally occurring at scales enormous and little, from roof sunlight based chargers on homes that can sell power back to the framework to goliath seaward wind ranches. Indeed, even a few completely provincial networks depend on sustainable power for warming and lighting. As sustainable use keeps on growing, a key objective will be to modernize America's power matrix, making it more brilliant, safer, and better coordinated across areas.

Coal, fossil fuel and diesel gas falls under as nonrenewable, or "messy," energy incorporates petroleum derivatives. Fossil fuel and coal sourced energy derivatives are two of the most non-renewable energy sources that amount to a huge environmental pollutants. Nonrenewable wellsprings of energy are just accessible in restricted sums and consume a large chunk of the day to recharge. At the point when we siphon gas at the station, we are utilizing a limited asset refined from raw petroleum that has been around since ancient times.

Besides, this type of energy sources are in obscure areas of the planet, making them more copious in certain countries than others. On the other hand, each nation approaches daylight and wind. Focusing on nonrenewable energy can likewise work on public safety by decreasing a country's dependence on sends out from petroleum derivative rich countries. Numerous non-renewable energy sources can imperil the climate or human wellbeing.

Fig. 9.3 Solar panels in array distributing electricity

Image Credits: https://pexels.com

For instance, oil boring may require strip-mining Canada's boreal timberland, the innovation related with deep oil drilling can cause tremors and water contamination, and coal power plants foul the air. To finish it off, this multitude of exercises add to an unnatural weather change.

CHAPTER 10
METAVERSE

Metaverse described as 3D virtual worlds mainly for social related activities and it is going to reshape how the internet is used in the future.

<u>Fig. 10.1 depicts a user gaming with Oculus</u>

<u>Image Credits: https://pexels.com</u>

With respect to futurism and science fiction, this refers to hypothetical loop of the Internet taking the form of a virtual world powered by the application of virtual and augmented reality devices such as the "oculus" The initial use of the term metaverse came in 1992 cartoon feature comic book called "Snow Crash". As of today, different variations of metaverse exists as software utility environments such as Virtual reality Technology. Two of the most challenging issues of metaverse are privacy (*where user biometric information data can be automatically collected without user consent*) and obsession (*for instance electronic game has been reported to be consequential with mental and physical or bodily harm*) with the technology.

Games (such as Second Life, Roblox, Active Worlds & Minecraft where 3 Dimensional images are super-imposed) and Entertainment industry are two of the most important areas where meterverse software applications will dominate.in the near future. Others will include advancing work environments results, rich multimedia environments, electronic commerce, house property presentation and of cos fashion.

<u>Fig. 10.2 depicts a student with Oculus</u>

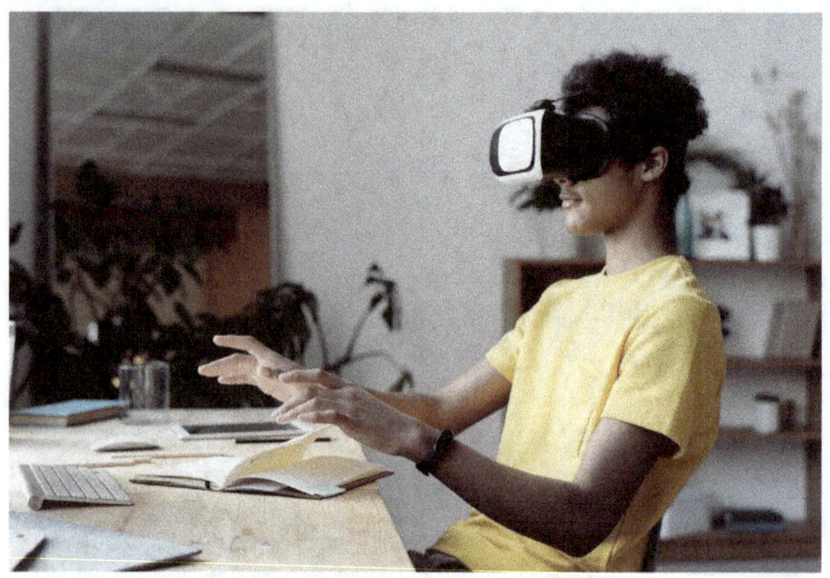

Image Credits: https://pexels.com

Virtual Reality software application contributes immensely to metaverse and companies such as Facebook, Microsoft (VR Firm known as AltspaceVR in 2017), and NVIDIA Corporation just to mention a few giant tech companies are all rolling out their own brand or variation of metaverse.

The major access points for metaverse software application will be Desktop and Laptop computers, phones, and similar devices drawing on the strength of Augmented and Virtual Realities.

Fig. 10.3 depicts a user animating with Oculus

Image Credits: https://pexels.com

For metaverse to become universally availed though, dependence on Virtual reality and high cost of display devices with high graphics and ease of mobility usage.

Fig. 10.4 depicts a user animating with Oculus Quest

Image Credits: https://pexels.com

Where you should focus your energy as far as Information technology is concerned is in the Open Extreme reality or OpenXR for short.

Several movies such as Marvel's Spiderman far from home (*Tom Holland*

and Jake Gyllenhaal), Ready player One (*Tye Sheridan*) and Blood Shot (*Vin diesel*) aptly show how metaverse will work in real-time.

and Jake Gyllenhaal), Ready player One (*Tye Sheridan*) and Blood Shot (*Vin diesel*) aptly show how metaverse will work in real-time.

REFERENCES

1. Sarma, Jyotirmoy and Guo, Zongqi and Dai, Xianming", Bioinspired photocatalytic hedgehog coating for super liquid repellency",Mater. Chem. Front, 2021, volume 5, issue 11, pages 4174-4181, publisher: The Royal Society of Chemistry.

2. The age of disruption: technology and madness in computational capitalism, Stiegler et al. - Polity Press – 2019.

3. Energy Efficiency Scheduling in Hadoop
Wenhong Tian, Yong Zhao, in Optimized Cloud Resource Management and Scheduling, 2015

4. Software Architect Bootcamp, 2nd Edition By Thomas J. Mowbray, Raphael Malveau Published Dec 10, 2003 by Pearson. O

5. "What Is Applied AI? | Cognizant." Www.cognizant.com, www.cognizant.com/us/en/glossary/applied-ai. Accessed 19 Feb. 2022.

6. "Future of Programming"
https://www.partech.nl/en/publications/2021/02/future-of-computer-programming#, Accessed 19 Feb. 2022.

7. "The Biohttps://www.weforum.org/agenda/2021/05/the-biorevolution-is-kicking-off-heres-how-to-harness-its-opportunities-early-on/

ABOUT THE AUTHOR

Owoeye Oluwatobi Michael is a graduate of Computer Science (B.Sc.), Transport and Logistics (M.Sc.) with postgraduate interests in **Robotics and Mobile Computing: Computer Vision, Machine Learning Distributed and Parallel Computing Algorithms**. He is also an entrepreneurial scientist whose passion and insight for problem solving pushes beyond current innovative technologies.

His first scientific publication released on the 15th of June 2013, the first in line of a series of technical books, which has touched several Department of Computer Sciences in the United States, Australia, Canada and United Kingdom. Over the past eighteen (18) years, he has contributed to IT infrastructural development in public and private organizations in Nigeria.

In March 2018, he was one of the finalists in the Next Einstein Forum competition of African Institute of Mathematical Sciences, held in Kigali, Rwanda where he presented a novel solution for healthcare in Africa. Besides, he is also the founder of Handsonlabs Software Academy.

57

63

Top Ten (10) Science & Technology Trends: Beyond 2022

73

Top Ten (10) Science & Technology Trends: Beyond 2022

75